Pace Bowling

SPORTING SKILLS SERIES

Pace Bowling

BOB WILLIS

WITH THE ASSISTANCE OF PATRICK MURPHY

PELHAM BOOKS

First published in Great Britain by
PELHAM BOOKS LTD
52 Bedford Square
London WC1B 3EF
1978

*Photographs by Ken Kelly (pages 8, 16, 17, 30, 31, 32,
35, 69, 74-5, 102, 116) and Patrick Eagar*

ISBN 0 7207 1093 6

Printed in Great Britain by
Hollen Street Press Ltd at Slough, Berkshire
and bound by Dorstel Press at Harlow Essex

Contents

Introduction

Since I was sixteen, I've been told my bowling is all wrong. My opening partner at school in Guildford had a magnificent run-up and delivery . . . yet he couldn't bowl fast. At the other end I'd be all jangling arms and legs, I'd be open-chested at the crucial moment of delivery, my followthrough was a coach's nightmare – *yet the ball left my hand quickly.* The one fundamental asset a quickie must have is the ability to whip his arm over quickly at the time he delivers the ball. I'll explain later how you need co-ordination of trunk, arms and legs to achieve vital rhythm, *but unless that ball leaves your hand quickly, you'll never make a fast bowler.*

Now I know I'm not exactly the kind of model a youngster should have if he wants to beat a good batsman by sheer pace. I'm aware of my own limitations – God knows I've been told about them long enough. My action puts great strain on a physique that's not especially well-developed. My style has put particular strain on the groin, ankles, the sides and the shoulders. Because I'm open-chested when I deliver the ball, I have to rely on the shine or the seam for the outswinger. But for some reason I can bowl fast. My height enables me to get extra bounce, I've come to appreciate the value of fitness, I've been lucky enough to get some good advice over the years, and as I got older I found some commonsense from somewhere and listened a lot more to people I respect.

And I'll say one more thing to the purist who wouldn't let Bob Willis loose in the nets on his young lad – I'm the only fast bowler in England of genuine consistent high speed. What's more I'm the only one to have come through in the last decade. I think that's

OPPOSITE *No matter how unorthodox the method, if the ball leaves your hand quickly, you've got the basic ability to be a fast bowler. The ball should be just a blur as it leaves the hand*

disgraceful, and when you think of our fast-bowling heritage – Tom Richardson, Harold Larwood, Fred Trueman, Frank Tyson and all the rest – it's ridiculous that it took a newspaper and a toilet soap firm to launch a competition in 1977 to try to find an English fast bowler worth coaching and encouraging. Young, strong lads have been scared off fast bowling for a variety of reasons, and while this dearth of fast men hasn't exactly harmed my Test career, I still envy the way the West Indians and the Australians seem to churn them out effortlessly.

And if you doubt the importance of fast bowling, just take a look at the Test match figures of the past decade. The decisive factor has almost always been fast bowling – think of the South Africans (Procter and Pollock against Australia in 1970), think of Snow for England against Australia a year later, then Lillee and Thomson rattling through England and West Indies in successive years, and what about the West Indian trio of Roberts, Holding and Daniel in England in 1976? It's the fast bowler who makes the decisive breakthrough in Test matches, even more so when he has to contend with a typical easy-paced wicket. He's the man his skipper turns to when he's lost the toss and demands something special to counteract the disadvantage of batting second.

In the field a Test match captain normally bases his strategy round the new ball – he wants to give his fast bowler a rest before taking it, and he needs a bowler to keep things quiet. This is where Derek Underwood and Max Walker have done such a good job in recent seasons: they've kept a break on the scoring while the strike bowler gets a second wind.

There's no respite when a fast bowler's operating at full throttle. If he's quick enough he'll be desperately difficult to score from, and with the new ball he can always come up with the unplayable delivery. It's a war of attrition, and the mental strain on the Test batsman is immense. Just look at the trouble England's batsmen had in 1974/5 against Lillee and Thomson – they'd get about twelve overs an hour, and after you'd taken away the bouncers (which English batsmen generally don't try to hook), the fast good-length deliveries and the wide ones, there were very few left to

OPPOSITE *You must use your height to make the ball bounce, an important part of the fast bowler's equipment on hard, fast wickets. My extra height means that with a final leap I can send a fast delivery down from well over seven feet – and I assure you no batsman likes fast, short-pitched bowling sent down from a great height*

9

score off. Then Max Walker would come on and seal an end up, hitting the splice of the bat rather than bowling bouncers, and by the time he'd done his stuff, Lillee or Thommo would be back refreshed and the ordeal would start all over again . . .

Whether you like it or not, that's the way successful Test sides structure their tactics in the field – and the core of the tactics is the fast bowler.

I'm often asked about the effect a quickie has on the crowd: do you feel the buzz from the crowd when you or another fast bowler come on, they ask? Well the answer's an emphatic 'yes'. The crowd love to watch a genuine speed man really slip himself. When you're watching the play side-on from the boundary, you see the bowler pace out what seems an amazingly long run, he comes tearing in, there's dust everywhere, a whirl of arms if there's a near thing, and all the time the slip and wicketkeeper are crouched, it seems, miles away. It's all-out attack, the big guns are out, it's almost gladiatorial. All the batsman has to defend himself with is a small piece of wood – and the crowd love the challenge thrown down by the genuine fast bowler.

I'm most conscious of this crowd feeling at the start of a Test if I open the bowling. I still get nervous, grip the ball too tightly, try to bowl too fast and get hooked off a slow long-hop that was supposed to be a demon bouncer, and then send down a full toss when aiming for the yorker. I'm caught up in the drama of it all and try to rush things instead of trying to find my rhythm – and if you examine my record you'll see I haven't always been able to make the vital early breakthrough.

So a fast bowler's a gladiator, he's an attacker, a player with a great responsibility to his team within the framework of the modern game. What other qualities must he have? He's got to be proud, resilient mentally and physically, he must be determined, optimistic, have a good memory and a lot of guts. I'll talk about these qualities in detail, but it's safe to say all the great fast bowlers of my time in the game have had these qualities. Yet they're worthless unless you've got that one vital asset – the ability to bowl fast . . .

It's extremely difficult to coach fast bowlers, in fact very few of

OPPOSITE *A sight the crowds love: the genuine fast bowler attacking top-quality batsmen – in this case Clive Lloyd facing Jeff Thomson, and at the bowler's end, Viv Richards. It's a spectacle, it's exciting, it's attacking, and the very lifeblood of Test cricket*

10

the coaches with counties or schools or top clubs have been quickies themselves. Fast bowlers really aren't manufactured, they're born. It doesn't matter how keen you are, natural ability's vital. Too many coaches talk about the Alec Bedser method of bowling – getting the back foot down and taking a huge delivery stride in one smooth rocking motion. But Alec Bedser wasn't a fast man, he was a great medium-pace bowler, and too often the Bedser style is worshipped without teaching the youngster *where* the pace comes from.

It's not a matter of sheer strength; looseness of limbs is more important, and the final rotation of the hips to give that vital propulsion which brings the bowling arm over fast. More about hips, propulsion, delivery strides and other such weighty matters later, but please, all you budding fast bowlers, just watch the opening bowler next time you're at a Test. His bowling arm will be a blur at the crucial moment of delivery. Remember Michael Holding's fourteen wickets at the Oval against England in 1976? Now that was a great piece of bowling on a dead track. How did Holding get all those wickets? By sheer *speed through the air* – never mind all the talk about seam and cut and swing, Holding beat the bat by speed *because his arm came over very quickly*.

So you've got to be natural to bowl fast. It's got to feel right, something I know from bitter experience. When I joined Surrey in 1969, I was a disaster at the start. The then coach Arthur MacIntyre kept on at me to change my action – he said I was too unorthodox and open-chested. I'll never forget my humiliation one day in the nets when I followed Arthur's instructions. I ran up, got my right foot parallel to the crease and the left near the batsman's blockhole in textbook fashion, swivelled as instructed at the right time, used my height correctly – *and the ball went into the side of the net*. It was all strictly according to the coaching manual, but the end product was hopeless. I began to get very depressed, and fully expected to get the sack at the end of the season. I couldn't even get in the second eleven, and my dream of playing for England looked a joke.

But I still thought I could bowl fast, and thankfully John Edrich did as well. Now I've got a lot of respect for Arthur MacIntyre as a coach – he's taught me a lot about fitness and discipline – but without Edrich I wouldn't have made the grade. I'd toil away in the nets at him for hour after hour, trying like hell to get the ball past the bat. It was like bowling at a brick wall, and if you beat the bat once in a while you'd live off that for the next half-hour. But Edrich, in that quiet way of his, took me aside one day and muttered: 'You can bowl fast, stick at it in your own style.' So I made do with the existing model and tried to build on that.

So one thing the young fast bowler needs is intelligent, far-sighted advice that doesn't adhere strictly to the coaching textbooks – and encouragement. Too many youngsters are put off by harsh, cynical words from those who should be encouraging them. If you're encouraged properly you feel more confident – and I've never seen a fast bowler bowl well when he lacked confidence.

The first thing I'd encourage a young fast bowler to do is to run up in practice and bowl as fast as he can. If he's quick enough you can build on that. A coach, though, must be able to spot the natural ability that's there, harness it, smooth off the rough edges but keep the vital asset of speed. But in my experience there aren't many coaches in England with this kind of knack.

Right, let's assume he's got natural speed. What then? A lot of hard work, for a start – and then some more. There's no short cut, you have to hammer away for hours at a spot to get that natural accuracy needed to survive in top-class cricket. I was scared stiff when I made the leap from club cricket to Surrey second eleven. Quite apart from the worries over my action, there was I, used to bowling about two hours a day, having to tear in and bowl all day in a three-day game! And then on the rare occasions I managed to pitch the ball on the wicket I'd get carted all over the Oval. You try to remain aggressive and do the things that were successful as a schoolboy, but it's a demoralizing experience, and unless you get in the nets and bowl for hour after hour and learn to pitch the ball on a length you haven't a hope.

As late as the 1974/5 tour of Australia I was bowling ball after ball at a piece of paper with Alec Bedser to recapture my line and length. And every fast bowler in first-class cricket has to do the same at some stage. And the only way to develop your bowling

13

Michael Holding shows how to beat and bowl a Test batsman when the wicket's dead and giving no help to the speed men. By sheer speed through the air Holding took 14 wickets in the Oval Test of 1976 – 9 of them clean bowled, a staggering percentage. The batsman experiencing that sinking feeling we all know so well is Tony Greig

When a fast bowler's lot is such a happy one: two occasions in the space of a couple of overs when I got everything right and blasted the man out by sheer speed. The unlucky batsmen are Barry Wood and Andrew Kennedy (left-hander) of Lancashire. I could look at pictures like these all day, especially if I was the bowler!

muscles is in the nets; you can't do that in the gym. It's taken me a long time to get myself really fit and to think about my body – I recall Ian Chappell saying in 1974 that if a batsman stayed in after lunch against me I was there for the taking. It hurt but he was right. I wasn't strong enough, and used to blow it early in the day by trying to bowl too fast.

Our Trueman of the future must be ambitious – like Fred, he really should expect a wicket every ball, he must get a shot of adrenalin when he knocks a stump out of the ground. A top-class batsman hates losing a stump – it's ignominious, there's no room for doubt, he's been well and truly blasted out, and I can tell you it's a great, masculine, overwhelming feeling if you're responsible.

The fast bowler's got to have 'devil': he doesn't want to see the

16

batsman badly injured, but he wants to tickle his ribs with a fast one to see him wince, and watch him rub the sore part. It's a straightforward contest, and the fittest and strongest has a good chance of coming out on top. No matter how soft he is off the field – and I've known many quiet, easy-going fast men once they're in the bar – he's got to have fire in his belly when he gets the ball in his hand.

It's hard work being a fast bowler, but it's also a tremendous thrill when things are going well. You feel right, you're revelling in the responsibility of being your team's main strike bowler, and you know the side's behind you. On days like that, it's the greatest feeling I've experienced. Let's now take a detailed look at the qualities needed to be a fast bowler . . .

B

1 Aptitude

Before a budding fast bowler can even *think* about mastering techniques and developing his skills, he's got to consider one vital question: can he bowl fast? I am afraid many think they are quick when in fact they are not much more than medium-pace. There is no point in deceiving yourself – if you can drop your pace and swing the ball and think: 'This is more fun, I don't work up a sweat until six overs,' then stick to medium-pace because fast bowling does not suit you temperamentally or physically.

It is *potential* I am considering now – forget the smooth, integrated finished product for the time being, what I want to know is: has he got the basic physique and ability for the task? Fast bowlers' physiques, of course, vary: there are the smallish men (for example Lindwall, Larwood, Trueman) and tall ones (Holding, Hall, myself) and the ones in between (like Snow, Thomson or Roberts). And the speed comes from different areas for different bowlers – a man like Lillee or myself will get it from a long, fast run-up, while a muscular fellow like Thomson gets it from the chest and shoulders.

But irrespective of physique – and I am assuming that someone under average height has realized he lacks the basic attributes to bowl fast consistently – the potential fast bowler should be well coordinated and athletic. He must be able to move smoothly: it does not matter if, for the moment, his action is awkward, but if he can run or turn easily and swiftly, he has the basics right. You can often tell this when a fast bowler's fielding – a man like John Snow, whether or not he was having one of his sonnet-composing daydreams, always looked smooth, athletic and coordinated, and you could see these qualities in his bowling.

When assessing ability in a young fast bowler, the place to judge him is out in the middle, not in the nets, where you can't get a true picture of him. Normally there isn't room for a proper fast bowler's run-up there, and if they are indoors he would be silly to go flat-out because the concrete floor puts a great strain on ankles and legs. When someone with potential is bowling in the middle I like to wander round the ground and view him from all angles. From behind his arm I'll be able to see if he can use the crease to vary the angle, and from side-on I can tell if his arm movement is swift enough, if that final exciting explosiveness is there. From side-on you can also tell if he's following through properly or just stopping at the crease when letting the ball go.

Whether you are an ambitious club cricketer or a youngster with potential, just remember it is a hard school a fast bowler is trying to enter, and even if he has the basic potential he won't make it without luck, encouragement and good coaching. It is so important to encourage fast bowlers – if he sends down five bad deliveries in a row and the sixth is a good one, then concentrate on that last ball and encourage him to discover the method of bowling it more consistently. A shy, spotty fifteen-year-old with real potential can be easily put off by a harsh word from a bored, cynical coach.

The promising young quickie must also be lucky – lucky with injuries, lucky with his school or club, and lucky with the coach who tries to shape him. I was noticed because I was uncomplicated, confident and bowled fast. My head wasn't crammed with theories, I just made the ball fizz through the air, in fact it wasn't until I joined Surrey that I realized my action wasn't textbook standard.

I'm not a great fan of cricket coaches in this country from a fast bowler's point of view. For a start there are hardly any – one of the reasons why I'm the only world-class English quickie to emerge in the last decade. A fast bowler is an athlete, he has got to be trained almost like a racehorse, and his coach must be nearly a physio-therapist as well as a psychologist. He must try to assess whether the boy fast bowler will grow any more. My own case sums up the

Dennis Lillee showing that explosiveness and huge final stride that's so important if you want to generate real pace – and this side-on position is the best from which to judge if the young bowler has the necessary potential

The importance of the
follow-through, as
demonstrated by Jeff
Thomson, Dennis Lillee
and a certain bowler whose
name escapes me. . . .
You mustn't stop at the
crease after delivery and
admire your work: you
must follow through
strongly. If both feet are
still on the ground, then
you're not putting enough
into the follow-through and
therefore not bowling fast
enough.

dilemma – I shot up from 5′ 6″ at fourteen to 6′ 4″ at sixteen. I was a beanpole, as thin as a matchstick, but luckily nobody stopped me from trying to bowl fast.

I think most coaches don't realize how much stamina is needed to manage the huge leap from school or club cricket to county second eleven standard. A club cricketer playing just weekends has to change from bowling two hours on Saturday or Sunday to perhaps four hours a day with a county – and it's even more demanding for a sixteen-year-old lad still at school. Most of the coaches just aren't up to dealing with fast bowlers – one good reason being that the majority of them were all-rounders and batsmen in their time, not fast men.

Just look around England and find me a young, genuinely quick bowler likely to play for his country. Where are they? Consider the case of Yorkshire. Now you would think with their vast coaching network and their tradition they would come up with a fast bowler or two. Anyone with real potential gets a run out in the Yorkshire second eleven – but they haven't thrown up *one* genuine fast bowler in years. And this is a county that contains a third of England's cricket-playing population!

Now I know some kids make it difficult for a coach trying to guide them on something as specialized as fast bowling. I honestly think there isn't the dedication among fifteen-year-olds that there was even when I was at school. Too many of them aren't fit enough for a start – quite a contrast to my time spent coaching in South Africa, where I found the boys very well-disciplined and eager to listen. But a good coach earns respect by being approachable yet still authoritative. How many times have you heard a coach tell a young quickie: 'Slow down, you're bowling far too fast,' give him a short lecture on the value of line and length, and then *discourage* him from trying to build up his pace again?

Right, that's enough on what harm can be done *to* a budding fast bowler; a word now on the harm he can do to *himself*. If he thinks he knows it all, if he reckons his coach is an old fool still living in the W. G. Grace era, then he can forget about making the grade. Every great fast bowler I've known could listen to advice

24

from people he respected. He must also watch other fast bowlers, sift through all that he's seen and heard and then apply the relevant parts to himself.

I've always been an avid cricket watcher – in my first Test series in Australia I watched *every* ball, and even now I try to see as much as possible. During a county match I like to stroll round and watch a particular bowler who can perhaps teach me something. I was lucky at the start of my career at the Oval: my second eleven skipper, David Gibson, told me what to look for, and Geoff Arnold was always fascinating to observe at close quarters – I always admired his smooth approach to the wicket. Then on my first Australian tour I played with three very good fast bowlers – Ken Shuttleworth with his classical action, Peter Lever building pace from his long run-up, and John Snow with his loping, easy style leading to great speed off the track. I made a point of watching the great Dennis Lillee on his first tour here in 1972, then Thomson and Lillee in Australia in 1974/5, and of course Roberts, Holding and Daniel on the West Indian tour of 1976.

Fast bowling is such a delicately poised art that you can lose something vital from it at any time. That's when you must rely on your own memory of watching others and also seek advice from people you respect. Now in fitness matters I've received many good tips from non-players, but when it comes to the art of fast bowling the only people I listen to are those with first-hand experience of top-class cricket. I've had some terrific advisers. One of them, the next man to shape my career after John Edrich, was Ray Illingworth on the 1970/1 Australian tour he skippered.

I had been flown out as a replacement and was still very raw. And until my first Test at Sydney I'd thought the right length to bowl fast was the same, i.e., just short of a length. But Graham McKenzie kept using his long reach to get onto the front foot and drive me. Ray said: 'Drop it back a yard,' and sure enough, McKenzie could not play me so easily. It had never occurred to me that you should alter your length according to the batsman's height. It seems so obvious now – a good-length ball to, say, Tony Greig is almost a bouncer to a little fellow like Alan Knott – but

Ray was the first man to tell me that. He demonstrated the value of encouragement; he could have given me a few rockets early on, but he kept giving kind, sensible advice so that I really wanted to bowl my heart out for him.

Then there's Tony Greig. Now it may surprise some of you who think Greig is flashy and a bad tactician, but he, more than anyone, has made me the bowler I am. He was terrific to me on the 1976/7 tour of India and Australia. He told me I was to be the main strike bowler and I relished the responsibility. His intense will to win rubbed off on me, he was approachable, and as a bowler himself and a batsman who'd faced all the great modern fast men, he knew about fast bowling. I really wanted to pull out something special for Greig – an hour would go by in a Test and we hadn't taken a wicket, so I knew that my extra pace would be needed to try for the breakthrough. It was a great feeling and I couldn't get enough of it.

Greig was also a shrewd tactician and psychologist. When he lost the captaincy he still helped me tactically, and he continued giving some great advice – he'd come charging up from slip, saying things like: 'You're hurrying back too much to your mark,' or: 'Try him with the bouncer.' I recall a couple of times when I bowled badly at Rick McCosker, the Australian opener. He was clipping me through midwicket because I was bowling at the stumps, making him play but letting him use his strong legside game. It was Greig who told me to aim outside his offstump.

David Brown, my Warwickshire team-mate, was another whose advice has been valuable. Behind the legpulling banter we always respected each other's abilities, and he helped me rationalize my role as strike bowler in the side. It wasn't important to bowl maiden after maiden – my job was to get wickets, to have 3 for 41 at lunch rather than 0 for 14. It's disappointing to concede nearly four runs an over, but Brown made me aware that a strike bowler must always aim for a wicket, not play a batsman in.

A coach, mentor or guide must always be approachable, and one man with that quality is Alec Bedser, for so long the chairman of England's selectors. You might only want five minutes with Alec but he'd always give you twenty-five, and then it was up to you to sort out what he'd said and then apply it to your own game. Bedser's a stickler for the old-fashioned ideals and techniques – hard work in practice, chopping down trees to build up the back muscles, bowling at one stump for hour after hour, running around fields with heavy army boots on to build up fitness. He's given me good advice on all things to do with fast bowling – from the action to training to the right food and drink.

Ken Barrington is another England official who's advised me well. On the two tours he managed – to India, then Pakistan and New Zealand – he was so enthusiastic he was almost like a player. He handled me just right: when I was bowling well, he'd say so during the interval, he'd boost me up – 'This bloke's scared stiff of your bouncer' – or advise me to be a little more careful – 'Don't overdo the short stuff, he's picked you off with some good shots.' And when I bowled badly, he'd leave me alone. Kenny knew I realized I hadn't bowled well, and he would keep quiet at the right time. And his credentials were excellent – a great player of fast bowling, he understood what made me tick. I'm grateful for the quality of advice I've received but I had the commonsense to keep my mouth shut and ears open at the right time. Fast bowling was the first thing I ever worked at; as a kid I was notorious for jacking in anything that needed concentration or hard work. But with cricket I soon realized the importance of listening, watching and looking after my body.

2 Physical Preparation

The average county cricketer just isn't fit enough for his job. He doesn't really want to know about trying to improve his stamina, and when it comes to understanding how much hard work's involved for a fast bowler to get properly fit, he hasn't got a clue. International cricketers – particularly those who've been on tour – realize that a quickie has to nurture his body, prepare himself for the immense strain involved in playing county cricket and touring in the winter. But the rank and file in the county game have a mental block about fitness.

Until halfway through the 1976 season I was the same: I was fit enough to play first-class cricket, but not to bowl consistently fast. I was lazy; if there was a way out of training I'd look for it. True, I'd suffered some bad injuries. My mind was playing tricks on me – I wanted badly to get fully fit but didn't want to work too hard at it in case of breaking down again through trying too much. But then two things in the space of eight months completely changed my attitude. First I saw the controversial intimidation from Andy Roberts and Michael Holding against the English batsmen at Old Trafford – at that time all England seemed to be moaning about the lack of a fast man to return the West Indian blitz. A newspaper and a toilet soap firm sponsored a competition to find a young English fast bowler, and I suddenly thought: 'What the hell, they've got one here already – me!'

Even though I'd only played three days' cricket in six weeks, I was chosen for the next Test and picked up eight wickets. I then realized how much I meant to the England team, and even more importantly what the England team meant to me. I'd really thought of packing it in earlier that season. I kept breaking down with niggling injuries, and I honestly thought bowling flat-out was putting too much stress on my body. I'd spent the previous winter resting at home instead of coaching in South Africa because I wanted to recover from the traumatic season of 1975, when a knee operation kept me out for all but the last three matches. But the rest didn't do any good – and until that Old Trafford Test I was heading for the fast bowling knacker's yard.

I had a good tour of India, getting gradually fitter and stronger, and then came the second decisive moment. After the Centenary Test against Australia, Tony Greig had a go at me at, of all places, a barbecue in Sydney. He said I'd run out of steam at a crucial time in the Test and that we might have won if I'd been fitter. I clutched at straws in my usual manner, muttering the obvious excuses, but he was right. Luckily another man at that barbecue was an old friend from a previous tour, Dr Arthur Jackson. Arthur's very good on fitness, and he said my training just wasn't good enough. The only way for me to get fit was by running. He gave me a book by the German coach Ernst Van Aaken containing training methods and diet advice. And since that day in Sydney, I haven't looked back . . .

The Van Aaken method was a vital ingredient in my success against the 1977 Australians. His running schedule means I am more resilient, I can concentrate on my bowling more and I've got the reserves of energy for that crucial period after tea. In the Trent Bridge Test I got five wickets an hour either side of tea and I could bowl a seven-over stint in the closing session instead of my usual four. My team-mates pull my leg about my running obsession, but my first injury-free season was in 1977 – when I took up the running programme.

And there's no mystique about it – basically it's all about running long distances slowly to build up endurance. I run half an hour a day in and out of season, anywhere I can – at the Edgbaston ground, in the park, in a wood or on a road. A word of encouragement for the club cricketer or youngster starting out on this course – it's very

One example of the strain suffered by fast bowlers. In 1974, my left knee was still fairly straight and it could take the weight at the time of delivery. Three years and two knee operations later and I've had to adjust the position of the left leg to avoid buckling

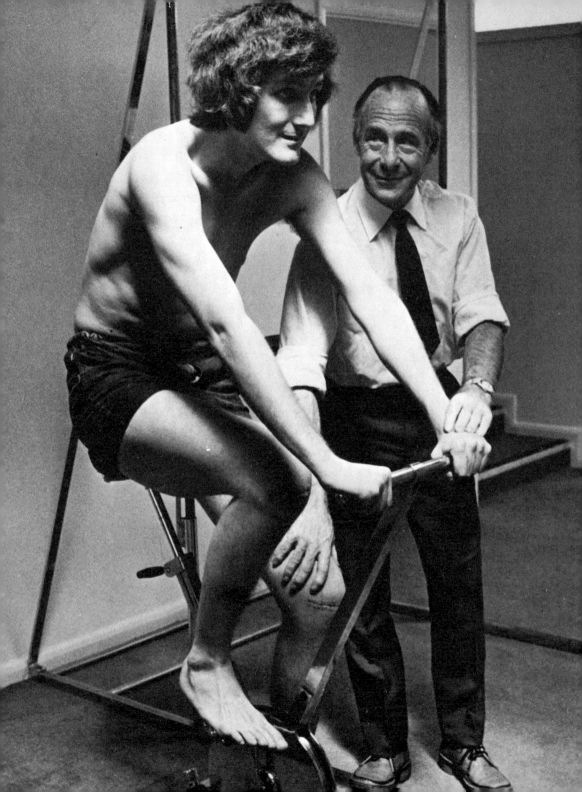

hard work at the start, so make do with fifteen or twenty minutes a day at first. You'll gradually build up stamina, and you'll be surprised how easy it becomes and how much you look forward to it. During the season I'll have my run an hour and a half before play's due to start, then I'll shower, change, do my other exercises, loosen up, keep warm – by which time it's the start of play and I'm really *ready* to bowl.

The running programme's helped in so many ways. It's disciplined my breathing, so that when I'm walking back to my mark I'm taking in the air at the right time, it's calming me down, so that when I run in, I'm relaxed and can build up that vital speed. It's strengthened my heart and lungs as well, vital areas for a fast bowler. Since I started training I've consistently felt better than any other time in my life. My confidence compared to those dreadful earlier days is amazing – and I'm a much better fast bowler too.

Another man who's helped me stop worrying about injuries is Bernard Thomas, the Warwickshire and England physiotherapist. Now Bernard may not know the difference between an off and a leg cutter, but the stretching exercises we do together have been invaluable. They've toughened me up in traditionally vulnerable areas – the hamstring, the back, the stomach muscles and the groin. His methods are simple and effective – the programme lasts fifteen minutes every morning after I've had my half-hour run. Bernard supervises in his best parade ground manner – 'To the left, two, three, four, to the right, two, three, four' – and the stretching loossens up the body remarkably. You intersperse it with light jogging to keep the limbs supple – rather like the methods used by the South American footballers.

When Bernard's not around I do the stretching exercises myself, and after it's over I feel loose, athletic and very fit. It never bothers me when my team-mates ask about my ballet classes because I know the exercises have helped make me a world-class bowler. I trust Bernard's diagnosis of my injuries, and he knows I need to be led – he can see if I've had too much beer the night before when we're on an England tour, and he's got the knack of making you feel small if you're not pulling your weight in the exercises.

OPPOSITE *Bernard Thomas, the England and Warwickshire physiotherapist, a man who's greatly helped my physical-fitness programme. Here he is, using that special mixture of parade-ground bluffness and charm to get me working on the bike after operations on both knees in 1975. And I've still got the scars to prove it*

C

33

The beauty of the Bernard Thomas/Van Aaken methods is that anybody can do them. No matter what standard of cricket you play in, these methods will make you a fitter and a better player. Just remember to have a shower and a change of clothing after your half-hour run. And don't run if you've got a cold: it'll affect your breathing. And if you're tempted to jack it in, just remember this – if a lazy bloke like me changed his habits, so can you. And if your mates laugh at you, console yourself that I suffered too – and I'm the one with over a hundred Test wickets, not the leg pullers.

Right, let's assume our fast bowler's stopped boosting the breweries' profits and got into the habit of running in the fresh air. He presents himself, bright-eyed and glowing with health, at the nets. What then? Well as far as I'm concerned, don't expect to bowl too much at a batsman. If you're genuinely fast the wickets in the nets are just too dangerous – even at Test ground level. And an average batsman feels claustrophobic in a net against a bowler who frightens him, especially if the uneven bounce means he's worried about getting his teeth knocked out.

In practice a fast bowler must learn to use his own initiative to improve his line and length. Get a box of balls and a single stump and bowl at that – and don't always put the stump in the centre hole; vary the line and remember the off stump should be your natural target. It takes far more discipline to bowl on your own for long periods than to lark about in the nets with your mates, concentrating more on the next quip than on what you need to improve.

So the fast bowler's now fitter, more accurate, with greater stamina, he's raring to go. But he can still throw all those advantages away if he eats the wrong food. He should aim for a good nutritional diet with plenty of protein and as few carbohydrates as possible. If you eat too much of the wrong sort of food, you get sluggish, you can't manage that important spell after tea, and you're not much use to your side. I normally have two boiled eggs for breakfast, skip lunch if I'm bowling that day, and eat well at night.

As for drink, many people still believe the myth about fast bowlers downing pints of beer during the interval and then breezing through the batting. Well, I've never seen a Test player drinking

OPPOSITE *How to pass the time before going on an England tour. The torture chamber is Bernard Thomas's gym in Birmingham, the facial expressions distinctly true-to-life*

34

Two examples of the strain involved in bowling fast for long periods. Mike Procter, a man who never stops trying, puts enormous strain on his neck muscles and right shoulder by bowling off the wrong foot, and his long final stride before delivery puts great pressure on his groin. Even that magnificent athlete Graham McKenzie suffered physically in the day-to-day grind of county cricket. Note the strain on his neck muscles and shoulders and the great stress placed on his left side when it has to take the extra weight at the moment of delivery. A pinched left side is a continual, nagging injury that bothers fast bowlers. One odd thing about the McKenzie picture – he's bowling round the wicket, something few fast men attempt in case they lose their rhythm beer during a day's play. I drink cups and cups of tea – there's nothing more refreshing – and if abroad on tour, we have soft drinks containing salt to replace that lost in sweat. Of course a few pints after the game are expected, but again you've got to use your commonsense. Before you imagine I'm busy adjusting my halo, let me assure you I was as self-indulgent as anybody. Before I buckled down to reality I was fifteen and a half stone, my flannels were tight on me, and I just wasn't properly attuned to my job. I'm now down to fourteen stone, the fast bowling machine's sleeker, and my career's been saved.

Yet even though a fast bowler's looking after himself correctly in his private life, in the gym, in the nets and on the running track, he's still vulnerable because of the terrible demands placed on his physique. His skipper wants him to turn a score of 200 for 3 at a quarter to six to 215 for 7 at the close, and so he strives, he strains, he forgets the stiff back he's got from standing in the shade after his previous stint – he's got the new ball in his hand, he's the potential matchwinner. Is it any surprise that we sometimes bowl ourselves into a bad injury?

You'll know in your own heart just how serious the injury is – and if it's a bad one you mustn't play again until it's gone. A batsman or another type of bowler can carry an injury, but not a fast bowler, he gets found out. Some of my worst ones have come from returning too soon. I remember a Gillette Cup semifinal against Lancashire. I'd burst a blood vessel two days before in a Test and should never have played. But my fellow fast bowler David Brown was doubtful for the match, so I thought: 'We've got so far, we've got to get to the final,' I played – and it was a disaster. I managed only three effective overs, I was a liability to the team, and we lost badly.

It's all so much easier if you're fit – and I mean *really* fit. Your feet may be killing you, a stud may be coming through, your toes probably feel as if at least three are broken and four amputated – but you'll get through if you *know* you've got the stamina and the high morale that comes from glorying in your fitness. It's as much a mental fitness as a physical one.

3 Mental Preparation

If you want to be fit enough for fast bowling at Test level, you've got to be mentally strong. Now I know lots of weekend cricketers will probably look at that statement and think: 'Here we go again, making the simple act of fast bowling look like a Freudian melodrama' – but a world-class fast bowler is someone who's relaxed mentally and physically because he knows that when necessary he can pull out a performance that wins a Test.

It wasn't till I was hypnotized by my good friend Dr Arthur Jackson that I became capable of consistently fast, successful bowling at the highest level. He gave me the mental strength that leads to that vital fitness. Now I don't want to upset my friends in Fleet Street, but the revelation that Arthur helped my career, leading to headlines like 'Hypnotism Helped Willis Skittle the Aussies', made me smile ruefully. The newspaper stories made it look as if I was some kind of zombie sent out by a Svengali, programmed to knocking over the Australians. That wasn't so, and Arthur was the first to admit it. What he did was form part of a programme that helped me bowl better than at any stage in my career.

The hypnotherapy – and here I must it stress was just one twenty-minute session – was designed to bring home to me the importance of Van Aaken's running programme. Arthur was an old friend of mine, and he knew that I tended to give up at crucial moments, blaming an injury or the wicket or anything convenient. After the Centenary Test in March 1977 I asked him to help me with my

39

insomnia. I realized my tenseness wasn't helping my bowling development, and after that twenty-minute session I felt better straight away. I was more relaxed, less talkative, more self-contained and more confident. And he had instilled into my subconcious the importance of a controlled, planned training routine.

I realized I'd get nowhere in big cricket without striving to become extremely fit. I buckled down to the Van Aaken programme as soon as I returned to England, and I never looked back. No longer did I run myself down, I stopped telling everyone that naturally talented bowlers like Mike Hendrick and Chris Old had more to offer England than me, and I matured. I still play the tape of that fateful hypnosis session when I want to relax and be on my own. It helps concentrate my mind and sort out the priorities. But it's no more sinister than that – sorry to spoil a good story, lads, but I'm not yet a candidate for the headshrinker's couch.

Once self-discipline became an integral part of my life I was bound to improve. My new-found mental resilience meant I was fitter, and once this was added to my tactical memory I was on my way. Now if there's one asset I'll unashamedly claim it's a good memory for batsmen's weaknesses. I think that's very important for a bowler of my type – a naturally gifted man like Mike Hendrick or Geoff Arnold could bowl the outswinger at will, whereas I had to work at my craft. So I had to do my homework more thoroughly.

A good bowler – irrespective of his pace – must always study the technique of good batsmen, file away his impressions and then use them to his advantage. I was taught this in the early days at the Oval by Ken Barrington, who told me to keep a notebook of individual batsmen's weaknesses. I remember he pointed out to me that Mike Smith of Warwickshire used to get into a bad position on the back foot early in his innings, so Kenny would encourage me to bowl a long half-volley at his off stump. I thought that intelligent tactics, and since then I've always studied other players.

At Test level I really enjoy hatching traps with my team. I can think of many examples where long-term planning's worked. There was Greg Chappell, the Australian skipper in 1977 and a magnificent batsman. He was obviously the danger early in the series, and

40

we decided at a team talk that I'd try to trouble him with a few fast bouncers at the Old Trafford Test. Well, he got a hundred in that innings, but I unsettled him so much that he was never the same player in that series. He was unnerved by my pace, didn't get properly into line in subsequent innings, and I had him caught in the slips twice. I'd remembered what I'd read a few months earlier about Imran Khan's eleven wickets for Pakistan against Australia in Sydney. Chappell was quoted as saying that Imran had bowled quicker than anyone else in his experience in Australia. I thought to myself: 'I'm quicker than Imran' and made a mental note for the forthcoming series.

Another example: Rick McCosker, the Australian opener, is a fine player, but he is predominantly an on-side batsman. I studied him and bowled outside his off stump so he couldn't work me away to leg from middle and off.

My ability to file away relevant information means I bowl better against better batsmen. It's the supreme challenge, and since I became more relaxed about my fitness I've been able to concentrate on tactics. I think I have bowled very well against the prolific Australian Doug Walters. Now I know many say he's no use in England, but he's a very dangerous player once settled and I varied between bowling him bouncers (because he's a poor hooker early on) and the ball outside the off stump that he snicks to gulley. Sounds easy, but with a punishing player like Walters the margin of error is very small.

The West Indian Viv Richards is another example. He was in tremendous form in 1976 in England, yet I got him out twice in my comeback Test at Headingley; because of his leg-side excellence I had to bowl on the off side, but not wide enough to allow him to step back for the cut, another of his great strengths.

The fine Indian batsman 'Sunny' Gavaskar is the kind of player a bowler needs to study. He's an excellent judge of when to leave the ball alone and yet he's a rash hooker. So you dig the ball in around his breastbone (remember he's a small man), keep him tucked up on the back foot, and hope he'll get frustrated and sky a mistimed hook.

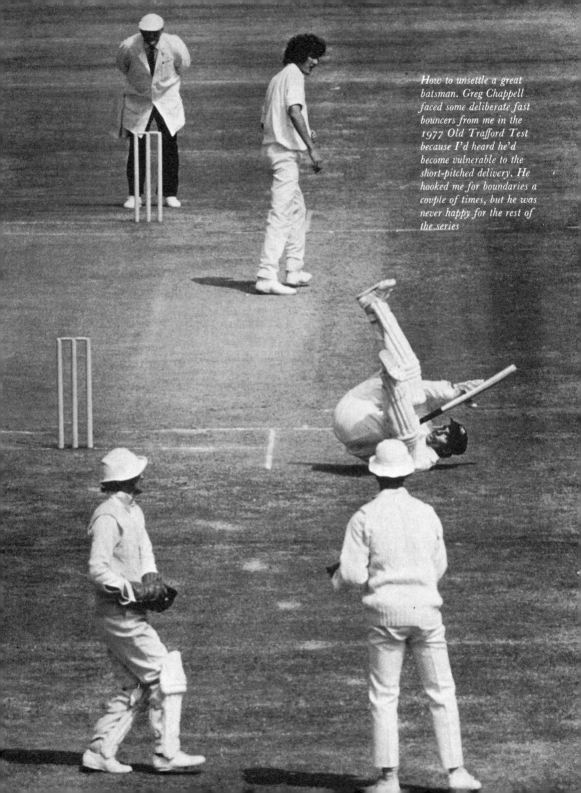

How to unsettle a great batsman. Greg Chappell faced some deliberate fast bouncers from me in the 1977 Old Trafford Test because I'd heard he'd become vulnerable to the short-pitched delivery. He hooked me for boundaries a couple of times, but he was never happy for the rest of the series

I find this mental approach fascinating and I enjoy poring over the county cricket scores in the papers. You can normally tell from a straightforward score card where a batsman was caught – you get to know the specialist close-in fielders, and if it's an unfamiliar name you can be fairly sure the batsman's holed out at long leg or mid-on or somewhere like that. In the county game, if you've got the inclination, you can profitably analyse a batsman's weaknesses because after a couple of seasons he'll rationalize his batting and accept his weak points.

The 'bush telegraph' on the county circuit is still very influential. Players from both sides often have a drink after a match and sometimes a plan to dismiss, say, Geoff Boycott is conceived by comparing notes. It's always trial and error, and more often than not it backfires, but it's enjoyable and instructive to sit down and think out the game. And it's amazing what you can learn from the average pro – I've known the time when I've played in a Test series and a county player who only watched it on TV will say: 'That bloke gets into a funny position for the hook shot doesn't he?' . . . and I might never have spotted it.

The fast bowler who learns from the county grapevine is maturing, and it's the same with a quickie who can stifle his frustration when he's bowling. It's no use waving your arms about and standing still with mock disbelief – if the umpire's turned you down or a catch has been dropped, get back to your mark, take some deep breaths and try to forget it. Easier said than done, I admit – and I'm still undisciplined if a catch goes down off my bowling. I occasionally stand there making sarcastic remarks about the elusiveness of that electric ball, stalk back fuming, bowl a rank long-hop that was supposed to be a bouncer, or simply bowl too fast.

Instead I should say to myself: 'I'm not going to do what that *** thinks, I'll bowl him a slower one.' You get caught up in the emotion of it all, but in my case the frustration only lasts one ball. Only once have I made a song and dance about an appeal being turned down. It was against Middlesex. Mike Smith, the opener, was so plumb out lbw on the back foot that he was almost walking

44

Jeff Thomson – an ideal temperament for a fast bowler. He gets on with the game, tries to bowl as fast as he can and doesn't sulk too much if a catch is dropped or a decision goes against him

to the pavilion. Imagine my amazement when the umpire said: 'Not out.' I went spare, I swore, ranted and raved and gave the sort of histrionic performance Fred Trueman would have envied. It was a disgraceful piece of behaviour which had no place in any class of cricket.

The fast bowler I admire in this respect is Jeff Thomson. If an appeal goes against him or a catch is dropped, he'll just come out with a good Anglo-Saxon curse, but he'll say it on the way back to his mark. He doesn't turn the episode into a dramatic interlude, but gets quietly on with the job.

4 Technique

Whether you are a schoolboy or a club cricketer, you'll never make a class fast bowler if you spray the ball about. It doesn't matter if you are supremely fit, psychologically resilient, with a natural fast bowling talent – without good control of the ball you are a liability to your team. It's the *art* of fast bowling I'm talking about now – what to do with the ball, when to alter your control and how to develop into the all-round skilful performer. It's the progress towards the day when you no longer panic after being hammered and think on your walk back to the mark: 'What on earth do I do now?'

How do you develop control? Regular net practice is vital. It takes years of practice to be able to deliver the ball where you want it at high speed. Early in my career, I was lucky enough to study John Snow's high degree of skill in controlled fast bowling. Time after time the batsman would be driven onto the back foot, unable to play the ball off the square. His hostile accuracy was not achieved by writing poems and thumbing his nose at the cricket establishment – he mastered it in the nets, year after year.

A fast bowler must hammer away, especially on a good wicket. He must try to get the batsman half back, half forward, to a ball fractionally short of a length on the off stump. That should be his stock ball and then, once the batsman is stuck in a groove, confuse him with slight variations of delivery. Make him play at every one, don't let him get comfortable. Some of the top bowlers in modern cricket have perfected these variations. Dennis Lillee is the master of that most dangerous ball, the outswinger, but Jeff Thomson's better with the yorker, the most dangerous surprise delivery in any standard of cricket. The best one I've seen was Thomson's to Tony Greig at Brisbane in 1974/5: it was deadly against a man with such a high backlift. Michael Holding also bowls a superb yorker – on the tour of England he bowled out many Test players.

Any self-respecting fast bowler should try to swing the ball through the air and get it to alter its line when it hits the seam. That way the batsman's kept guessing all the time. But remember one thing: the faster you bowl, the less swing you'll get. This is where the quickie must use his intelligence by following a really quick one with a slower ball that'll swing more. I'm not going to give you a lecture on the appropriate grips to adopt when swinging the ball. The normal textbook recommendation – point the seam towards leg slip for the inswinger and second slip for the outswinger – is correct. But the swing doesn't always follow that pattern. I remember Mike Brearley telling Mike Hendrick, a master of swing bowling, during a Test that he wanted three outswingers in a row followed by an inswinger. 'Sorry skipper,' said Mike, 'I don't know which way it will swing when it leaves my hand.' So don't be too upset if your intended late inswinger ends up hitting second slip on the knee. If you don't know where the ball's going, you can bet your life the batsman has no idea.

Looking after the ball is of paramount importance. Now I know we bowlers are often accused of cosseting the ball and rubbing it far too much, but you really must keep the seam dry and clean and polish one side of the leather to assist the swing. The seam should be the first part of the ball to hit the wicket – that way it will hopefully deviate off the pitch. If you get the ball back and find there are scuff marks on the leather part then you're not making proper use of the seam. Try not to grip the ball too tightly when delivering it – one of my faults early in my career, and something I still occasionally forget about. You should barely touch the ball at the moment of delivery, just have the first two fingers on either side of the seam with the thumb for balance. That way you've got more control of the ball, and the seam will hit the pitch first.

The run-up is one of the fast bowler's major problems. Every

OPPOSITE *John Snow demonstrates the ideal way to deliver the ball at speed. The tips of his fingers are barely touching the ball, with the thumb acting simply as a steadying agent, and the seam will hit the pitch first, thereby giving the ball a good chance of deviating. All fast bowlers get tensed up sometimes and grip the ball too tightly or lodge it firmly in the palm of the hand – resulting in a loss of pace.*
Snow's got everything right in this picture: his left leg is straight, his trunk has swivelled through ninety degrees at the right time, the bowling arm is high and the head is still, with the eyes looking straight ahead

48

quickie has troubles with this at some stage – I've chopped and changed time and again until I found the one that suited me. Unless you feel comfortable you won't do yourself justice. Don't worry about taking too long a run, provided it feels right. And if the end product is consistently fast, hostile, controlled fast bowling, you aren't likely to hear too many complain about the length of your run-up.

Wayne Daniel seems to waste his run-up by lumbering in a long way. Graham McKenzie and Len Pascoe have comparatively short ones. But in all cases, the last five or six strides are the decisive ones –that's when the final explosive surge leads to that vital speed of arm at the moment of delivery. Michael Holding has a marvellous run-up – a natural athlete, he glides in on tiptoe. The umpires say he is such a smooth mover that they cannot hear him approaching. You could never say that about Dennis Lillee – he's the greatest all-round quickie I've seen, yet he is curiously flat-footed in his run-up. That knees-up, pounding style of his surely jarred his body on the way in and put him slightly off balance, but the end product was good enough so he must feel comfortable.

I'll never forget when I first saw Jeff Thomson in Australia. He ran in slowly – similar to Bob Woolmer's approach – but then in the last few strides he'd pull back his right arm so that it nearly touched the ground, and the resulting speed was tremendous. Thomson's another who's athletically smooth, and his run-up is a lovely blend of relaxation and controlled explosion at the right moment.

What must you do if you lose your run? I think long-jump practice is useful; it helps time the sprint and stops you overstraining in the last few strides. The return crease behind which you should land is like the take-off board in long-jumping. But you mustn't look down, otherwise you'll be all over the place and off balance when you get to the wicket. But it's difficult on some grounds to keep your footing. Unlike long-jumpers, the bowlers have to negotiate undulating cricket fields, and it can be very difficult when you're worried about your bowling to try to streamline the run-up when accelerating downhill or straining uphill.

OPPOSITE *Wayne Daniel shows how to get the best out of the last few strides before the moment of delivery. Daniel's approach is a lumbering, ungainly one, but when it matters he uses his height and really whips his body round to produce that final explosive surge*

A contrast in run-ups. Dennis Lillee's approach is flat-footed and businesslike and the constant jarring on the run-up must surely put him slightly off-balance. Michael Holding's on the other hand is all liquid grace – he's gliding in, utterly relaxed and lithe, gathering momentum all the time while seemingly taking nothing out of himself. One other point – both men are looking straight ahead, if they were worried about their approach they'd have to look down and be completely off-balance when arriving at the wicket

PAGES 54-9 *The magnificent, unique action of Jeff Thomson. He pulls back his bowling arm so far that the batsman can't see the ball until the last moment. The huge final stride means he can rock back and use the shoulder power that makes him such a good javelin thrower. The strong left leg is braced at the right moment, the head sights the target over the left shoulder and the explosive follow-through is excellent. Perfect!*

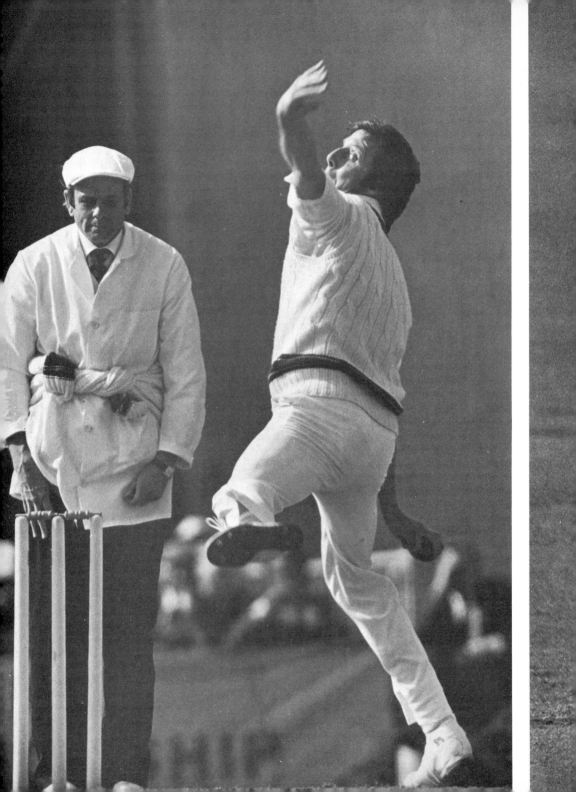

So let's assume you've got the run-up organized. Now it's the crucial moment of delivery, when all the power is channelled into getting that bowling arm to whip over as fast as possible. It's a case of getting the most from your action, and it comprises planting the rear foot parallel to the crease so that the hips will rotate through ninety degrees, keeping the head still so that the ball goes where you intend, and trying to brace the left leg to take the strain of the body swing. That's the classical recommendation, and if you can manage those basics you're on the way to bowling fast. But it's interesting to note how unorthodox the top fast men are. Dennis Lillee doesn't brace his left leg, Andy Roberts has a round-arm delivery. And there's the unique Mike Procter: he does not bother with a delivery stride, but seems to bowl in his run-up.

Then there's Bob Willis. I'm unorthodox myself, but like the other quickies I've mentioned in this book, I have one priceless asset – I get body swing by rotating my hips, and that's why I can let the ball go quickly. Frank Tyson, a man who knows all about fast bowling, maintains that the main momentum comes from hip rotation, from side-on through that ninety-degree turn. And it's amazing how this ability to bowl fast stays with you. Years after his England days, Frank Tyson still can bowl only one way in his coaching school at Melbourne – and that's fast.

I've already mentioned keeping the head still. Like a racehorse, a fast bowler tries to run the shortest distance (straight ahead) but if the head's rolling from side to side, the rhythm's not there.

Now the fast bowler's working on his technique and is ticking over nicely, what should he do if he's making no headway against a good player? He could try bowling round the wicket. This is something few of us do, mainly because we're worried about losing our rhythm and line. Mike Procter uses this technique intelligently, and so does Dennis Lillee, who gave an object lesson in this during a Test against England in Melbourne. Fred Titmus was leaving the bouncer well alone, by moving right over outside the off stump, so Lillee moved round the wicket, and as soon as this happened Fred was all at sea because of the different line and was soon caught in the gulley off a perfectly directed bouncer.

OPPOSITE *Long jump practice is very useful if you lose your run-up. It's the same principle, as demonstrated here by Dennis Lillee – you have to run a long way to a take-off board and time the jump exactly. The remarkable thing about this picture is the height of Lillee's left knee, considering he's run in at high speed. Note the left palm to the sky, the head over the left shoulder, the loose grip on the ball*

61

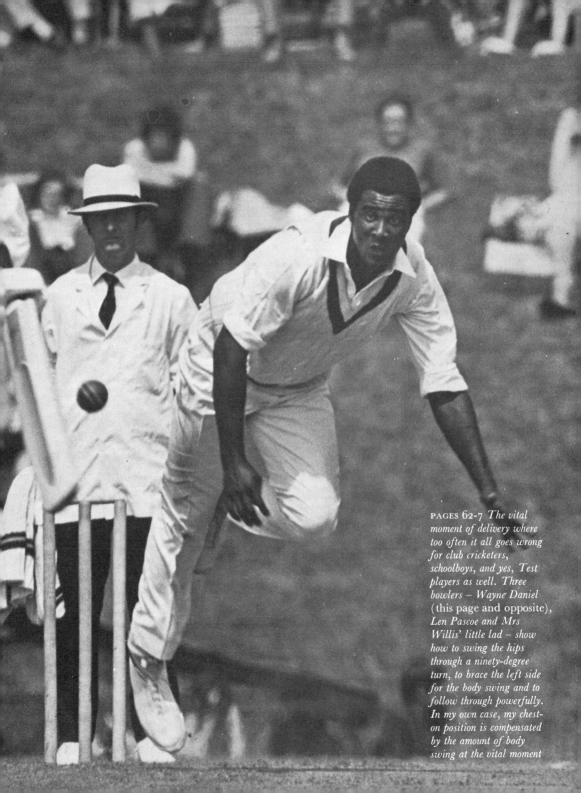

PAGES 62-7 *The vital moment of delivery where too often it all goes wrong for club cricketers, schoolboys, and yes, Test players as well. Three bowlers – Wayne Daniel* (this page and opposite), *Len Pascoe and Mrs Willis' little lad – show how to swing the hips through a ninety-degree turn, to brace the left side for the body swing and to follow through powerfully. In my own case, my chest-on position is compensated by the amount of body swing at the vital moment*

Bob Willis

THIS PAGE *The unique bowling action of Mike Procter. He sprints in, doesn't bother with a delivery stride and seems to bowl in his run-up. It may not satisfy the purists but the result is high speed. But Mike does one thing according to the textbooks – that final leap gives him the height to bang the ball in*

OPPOSITE *What a difference five years and a lot of advice makes. In 1972 my action was all wrong – I was off-balance when leaping into the delivery stride, my left arm (which is needed to steady the body) was too high, I gripped the ball too tightly, and because I bowled too wide of the stumps, I sprayed a lot of stuff down the leg side and my stock delivery was the inswinger. By 1977, I'd straightened out my run-up to get nearer the stumps and use the seam and swing to bowl an outswinger, the left arm was lower, giving me better balance, I was much more upright and used my height far better. And I was using just the tips of the fingers to guide the seam on to the pitch*

68

Not enough fast bowlers
try bowling round the
wicket to disconcert a
batsman who's well set.
The risks are great – you
can easily lose your
direction and rhythm but
the advantage is that the
ball's being delivered from
a different angle and in the
case of a right-hander,
across the batsman's body.
Mike Procter bowls very
well round the wicket – this
delivery got him one of the
wickets in his hat-trick in
the Benson and Hedges
match against Hampshire
in 1977

It doesn't always pay to bowl every ball at the stumps. The hard-wicket players of Australia or the West Indies are very good at clipping the ball on the off stump through midwicket, so you must try to get them fencing outside the off stump. Lillee again is a master at this ploy – he bowls such a good length just outside the off stump, then a wider one and the batsman will hypnotically follow it. He'll be playing outside the off stump away from his body with a packed slip field waiting for the edged stroke.

Another fast bowler's advice is that most controversial one, the bouncer. No batsman likes it. It unsettles them, especially at the start of an innings when they're trying to get a sight of the ball. I've seen fine players worn down by the bouncer over a period of time – people like Dennis Amiss, Brian Luckhurst, John Edrich, Keith Fletcher, and even one of the greatest of modern times, Greg Chappell. The art is to conceal their fear – if a quick bowler senses they're scared he should slip a couple more round their ears. Sounds hard, maybe, but it's a hard game, and if the batsmen are playing first-class cricket they've got to learn to live with the short pitched delivery. It's a hard ball, too, and I would advocate the use of protective headgear and forget what the purists might say.

One word to club cricketers on the bouncer – be very careful. The wickets in Britain are so variable that a bouncer can get a batsman ducking into a ball he thinks will get up but comes through under stump height. This is one case where I don't think club or schoolboy cricketers should ape the Test fast men. Bouncers on underprepared wickets aren't funny . . .

At first-class level, though, the bouncer is a wicket-taker and a deterrent against batsmen who are tempted to come onto the front foot on an easy-paced wicket. You've really got to dig the ball in on a slow wicket: I'm lucky because my height enables me to get bounce, but it takes a lot out of a bowler and should be used very sparingly. It's tempting to overdo them on a quicker wicket, something I was guilty of when younger and more easily perturbed by aggressive batsmen.

It can be humiliating if you're hooked for six off a bouncer because you've thrown the gauntlet down, you're the one who' attacking – yet you have to stand and watch the ball being picked out of the crowd. I well remember Doug Walters hitting me for a huge six off the last ball of the day to reach his century in a session at Perth, and Lawrence Rowe during his mammoth 302 at Bridgetown hooked me clean out of the ground. But the hook is a risky stroke – no English batsman plays it really well, and although the West Indians and Australians get lots of runs with the hook it still gets them out. The secret is to disguise the bouncer by not over-straining as you get to the crease. John Snow with his languid run-up bowls a superb surprise bouncer, rather like Brian Statham's. It would stay low enough to threaten the batsman, rather than the tennis-ball type that would balloon harmlessly over the head. Andy Roberts is also a superb bouncer bowler – he manages two types, a slower one and then a vicious faster one which usually takes the poor batsman totally unawares.

The slower ball is another intelligent device, but a very difficult one to master. Basically you hold the ball further back in the hand, but it takes lots of practice. You must try to run in at the same speed, so the batsman doesn't realize what's coming. I haven't perfected the art yet myself. Perhaps I need more practice!

The fast bowler must always think of composing an over suitable for the particular stage of the game, especially when the going gets tough. A fast bowler can get rattled if a tail-ender hangs around. He'll be slogging or blocking the straight ones and leaving the wide ones alone. My England team-mate Chris Old showed me how to tackle them. Chris bowls just the right way at them, he gets it chest-height, so they have to play, and this, allied to his natural outswing, means he gets a lot of tail-enders caught in the slips or by the wicketkeeper. Make the tail-ender play every time at the ball that rises, and remember it's the exception rather than the rule when he hits you for a boundary.

Chris Old, in fact, is a coach's dream. Everything he does is right – he looks over his left shoulder at the right time, his right foot's parallel to the crease, he bowls a good yorker, uses the crease to vary his line, rotates his hips fully so that he bowls a superb late out-swinger. The budding fast bowler couldn't follow a better model.

OVERLEAF *My bowling against tail-enders isn't always as successful as this time when I dismissed Andy Roberts. Too often we all succumb to the temptation to bowl too fast at them, so that they can leave a lot of wild deliveries alone*

73

Chris Old is very good against tail-enders: he makes them play all the time and gets them nibbling just outside the off stump with a ball slanted across them that they have to play. He taught me that the ideal length to a tail-ender is one just short of a length that gets up chest height

Chris Old is a model for all young fast bowlers who suspect there's something wrong with their action but can't quite put their finger on it. Chris gets all the basics right: he looks over his left shoulder just before delivery so that he knows

where he's aiming, his right foot is parallel to the back crease to give him the powerful hip-rotation needed to bowl a good outswinger, he gets both feet off the ground in his final leap and he uses the crease well to vary his line. And the follow-through isn't curtailed – it's smooth and controlled. And I'm green with envy!

5 Temperament

You'll never make a fast bowler if you start feeling sorry for the batsman when you've hit him. You've got to think and act aggressively all the time – the ones who fall by the wayside may have as much natural fast bowling talent as the ones who make it, but they lack that crucial aggressive, resilient, determined streak. Many fast bowlers I've known were split personalities – they'd spit fire and fury in the best Fred Trueman manner, yet be quiet and docile off the field. But they *all* wanted to be a success.

The fast bowler of any side should be resilient. When he's hit for a boundary he should try not to show how upset he is. I make a point of walking back to the mark as soon as I can, steeling myself to come up with a good delivery next time. But I must admit, I have got carried away – once in a Test in India the tail-ender Madan Lal slogged me for a boundary. Derek Underwood was at mid-on, and he said to me: 'Relax, keep calm,' but all I could say was: 'Give me that ******* ball.' The next ball was also slogged for another four, and I then realized I had to calm down.

You've got to have guts as well . . . and the higher the standard the more guts are needed. They are needed when you're really shattered on a hot day and your feet are killing you. It's ten to six and you know another four overs are needed with the new ball, or even worse, with the old ball, and you have to try to make that swing or fizz through the air. You know what's needed but your brain keeps telling your legs that you can't bowl fast any more that day. It's hard, but if you even *think* about throwing in the towel you'll never make a quality fast bowler.

78

I think this ability to keep plugging away at the fastest speed possible has always been one of my strengths. In one Test I particularly remember against Australia I had to bowl nearly twenty-two eight-ball overs in searing heat when Mike Hendrick pulled a hamstring in the second over. I took 5 for 61 that day.

A quickie will push himself even more for a skipper he respects. I certainly did for men like Ray Illingworth, Tony Greig and Mike Brearley. A good captain can get that little extra out of you without you realizing there was anything left. It's true that a fast man gets overbowled in modern cricket, but then it's up to the captain not to push him too much if the conditions are unhelpful. But fundamentally a fast bowler should always want to bowl; you don't get wickets brooding at long leg convincing yourself you're too tired to slip yourself.

I think most county players believe fast bowlers are hypochondriacs. It's true we allow injuries to prey on the mind and affect the confidence that's vital to bowl fast, yet others can get away with a bruised heel, a pulled hamstring or a strained groin, but not the fast bowler. I've never ducked out of a match because I just couldn't face it, in fact once I went into a Test strapped up like a mummy, but I'm sure many of my fellow pros have thought I was swinging the lead sometimes. But a fast bowler's a delicately balanced cricketer, and he needs to be understood. A good example of sympathetic yet firm captaincy came in the Centenary Test when Tony Greig had to deal with Chris Old's bad hamstring injury. He made it clear to Chris that he could not go off till the innings was over. Chris responded well, dropped his pace a little, but kept going magnificently.

A fast bowler must be optimistic. His job is to bowl sides out, *not* keep batsmen quiet with the kind of nagging, medium-pace stuff that's such a feature of the modern game. And he should be happy to use the bouncer whenever it's needed. He should not allow himself to worry if his bouncer hits the batsman. Of course, no one wants to see broken bones or blood on the pitch, but a fast bowler should be proud of his power within the rules of the game. I don't believe I'd ever get involved in the kind of intimidation

79

Brian Close and John Edrich had to suffer at Old Trafford in 1976 because I just don't think it's part of the game. I believe the point of bowling bouncers is to get batsmen out, and the futility of the Roberts/Holding effort was exposed because they didn't get anybody out that fateful evening.

But the bouncer is part of the fast bowler's armoury, and he mustn't be too soft to use it. I've known occasions when the fast bowler got carried away. There was Dennis Lillee in Australia in 1974/5: the crowd seemed to whip him into a fervour, and there were times in that series when he was like a man possessed. He even bowled a beamer at me in one Test, and I let him know in a fairly forceful way that I wasn't impressed. Then there was Vanburn Holder, the West Indian. He sent down five bouncers in one over against me. Vanburn was trying to win his Test place – it was a tourist game against Warwickshire – and I kept snicking and slogging him for boundaries, but I still thought it unnecessary.

Mind you, I think the English pace bowlers of my time have been too soft. I remember the Centenary Test, when we didn't quite know how to bowl at Rick McCosker when he returned to bat with his broken jaw in the second innings. I was the man who broke Rick's jaw in the first innings. He was a grotesque sight when he came out to join Rod Marsh. His face was terribly swollen, and he was swathed in bandages, but he proved he was competent by adding vital runs with Marsh. If the roles had been reversed I feel sure the Australians would have bouced him as soon as he came in again. Of course you admire the bloke's guts, but it doesn't mean you should make things easy for him.

Perhaps I can use my feelings when I bowled Rick in that first knock to show what a fast bowler's temperament should be like. When he played the ball on to his wicket off his jaw my first reaction was one of elation. He was a good player and I'd got him out cheaply, so I didn't take much notice of him staggering around. Afterwards I was sorry for him, but a fast bowler's job is to get a man out and then worry about the damage.

I believe bouncers should be bowled at everyone; I don't agree with the code of conduct that means the tail-enders should be

80

Dennis Lillee in a characteristic pose. A great crowd-puller, but there have been times when he's played to the gallery and overdone the bouncers and the aggro

allowed to build an innings that could prove decisive in the match. When I bat, I know how unnerving bouncers are, and I'll admit I get scared, but if necessary I'd wear protective headgear and expect others to do the same.

I'm worried about bouncers – I sincerely believe someone could get killed, and the memory will scar the particular fast bowler for life. I know my former England colleague Peter Lever was terribly upset for a long time after the New Zealander Ewan Chatfield nearly died in a Test after deflecting a bouncer onto his head. But surely anybody playing first-class cricket knows it's a hard game, and if he doesn't trust his reactions why not wear head protection? Why should a legitimate weapon in the fast bowler's list be out-lawed? I'm not saying there should be an all-out bumper war, but it's a wicket-taking tactic and batsmen should accept we're playing a hard, competitive game. I don't like knocking out batsmen – but let's keep things in perspective and remember two things . . . the batsman accepts the risk, and very few in first-class cricket misjudge a bouncer so they catch it on the head.

6 Support from the Team

A top-class cricketer is basically a selfish person. It's a game after all where the individual shines, and often a cricketer can forget his responsibility to the team while he's looking after his own interests. Yet a fast bowler in any class of cricket is a liability if he puts the welfare of the team to one side, if he wants to carry on too long or refuses to bowl because he's carrying an injury. It doesn't matter if the quickie's got all the attributes needed to get to the top – if he doesn't have the rest of the team behind him he won't consistently bowl fast and well.

The successful fast bowler in the club side, the school eleven or the county team must never forget he could have taken o for 60 instead of the matchwinning 6 for 24. Often a bowler doesn't bowl all that well, but brilliant fielding and catching rescues him and gives his analysis a flattering look. That kind of thing happens to all bowlers at some time, but it's at times like that when you realize how valuable team spirit is to your performance as the strike bowler. The England team under Tony Greig and Mike Brearley was a classic case: I really used to enjoy our team talks on the eve of the Test. Everyone, including the twelfth man, was encouraged to say his piece, and it was fascinating to see how much thought was going into beating the opposition.

I've mentioned how our team talks helped us tackle the great Greg Chappell. In the same series I bowled well against Max Walker after getting some good advice at a team talk. In the previous series against us, Max batted very well. He was allowed to

Dennis Lillee demonstrating something that every fast bowler at some stage forgets about — keeping the wrist cocked just before delivery and bowling with the palm facing the batsman. If the palm isn't straight on, the ball takes longer to get to the other end

get onto the front foot and use his long reach. But the next time I kept him pinned onto the back foot by bowling it just short of a length.

These eve-of-Test talks were great for team spirit. You really felt everyone was helping each other, and throughout the day's play someone was always giving the bowler a useful tip. I remember Tony Greig reminding me many times to keep my wrist cocked when delivering the ball. Unknown to me, the palm of my bowling hand was facing leg slip, and it was reducing my pace drastically. One word from Greigy and the wrist was high again and my speed was back . . .

Good team spirit is vital when a quickie's striving extra hard for the breakthrough against a tail-ender. He probably doesn't realize he's trying to bowl too quickly and a quiet word from a colleague often does the trick. But if the bowler doesn't welcome advice he eventually won't get any, and he'll be a lesser bowler because of that.

Team spirit can be judged by the quality of the fielding. That 1977 side was the finest fielding side I've played in – I picked up several wickets because of brilliant catching, particularly in the slips by Hendrick, Greig and Brearley. That kind of thing gives the quickie a tremendous lift. He forgets he's shattered, he thinks to himself: 'That was a bonus, because it wasn't a great ball. If I can just sort out my length I'll run through this lot.'

The captain's the man responsible for team spirit. You must respect him and want to pull out that little extra for him. He's got to know just how far he can push his quickie, how much time he needs to loosen up. The fast bowler is the matchwinner in modern cricket, but the skipper must ration his strength. There's no point in overbowling him just after tea when you want him back for a blast in the last half-hour. I'm always annoyed when I'm taken off – you should always want that extra over – but the captain should be firm at moments like that.

He should also give the quickie the field he wants. This will have been sorted out beforehand, but if the fast man wants a field alteration during an over the captain should be sympathetic, because if the bowler's not happy with his field he won't bowl well. Field placing can be very frustrating for the fast bowler. I'm always that one fielder short when I open the bowling. There's the eternal dilemma of wanting an early breakthrough and putting men in close catching positions – yet you don't want to have 0 for 20 off two overs when the ball hasn't gone in front of the wicket but down to the third man boundary.

On a good batting wicket, I'll start off with three slips, a gulley, cover, long leg, backward short leg, a man in the bat-pad position at short leg and a mid-on. It's all-out attack, I'm the strike bowler and my job is to get wickets. But what do I do when he keeps pushing me through mid-off? Do I stifle that run-scoring shot by taking away the bat-pad fielder and put him at mid-off, thereby losing a close infielder? If he keeps snicking me through the slips do I take away my third slip and put him at third man? What happens when he starts deliberately running me down through the spot where third slip was?

You begin to sense the batsman's growing confidence. After all it's a moral victory for him when a close fielder is moved back: he's spreading the field, he's now into double figures and he can tell the fast bowler's getting a little frustrated. That's when your captain and your fielders must help you – the captain with tactical suggestions and the fielders by alertness, so that the batsman really has to work for his runs.

If you fancy yourself against a particular player and you want to keep him at the striking end the fielder must be aware of this and think: 'He's not getting a run to me.' This is where someone like Derek Randall is so important in the England side. Time after time I've seen Test batsmen refuse very long singles against him in the covers because they were scared of being run out. That kind of thing really gives the bowler a boost – he thinks: 'Good, I've got this guy for another ball.'

In first-class cricket the standard of fielding is improving all the time. More sides are practising it, and it's no longer dismissed as something you can either do or not do well. I'm a great critic of the one-day limited-over game, but the pressures of that type of

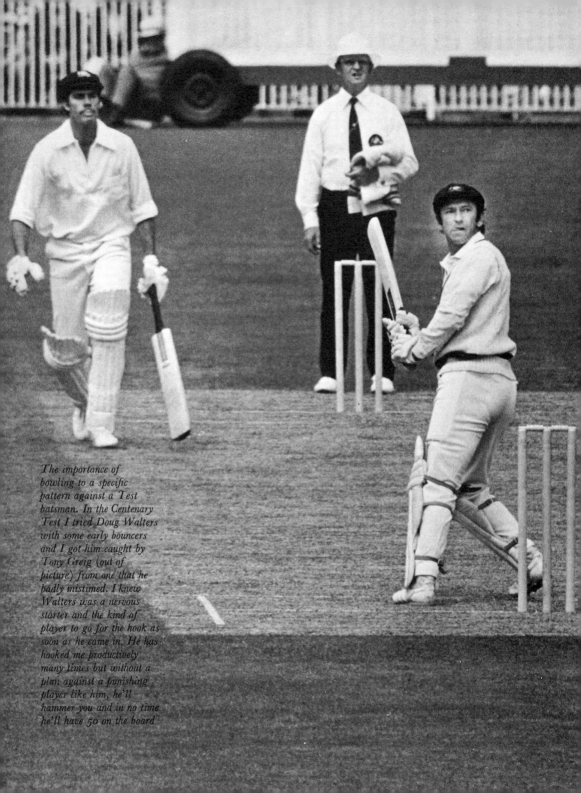

The importance of bowling to a specific pattern against a Test batsman. In the Centenary Test I tried Doug Walters with some early bouncers and I got him caught by Tony Greig (out of picture) from one that he badly mistimed. I knew Walters was a nervous starter and the kind of player to go for the hook as soon as he came in. He has hooked me productively many times but without a plan against a punishing player like him, he'll hammer you and in no time he'll have 50 on the board

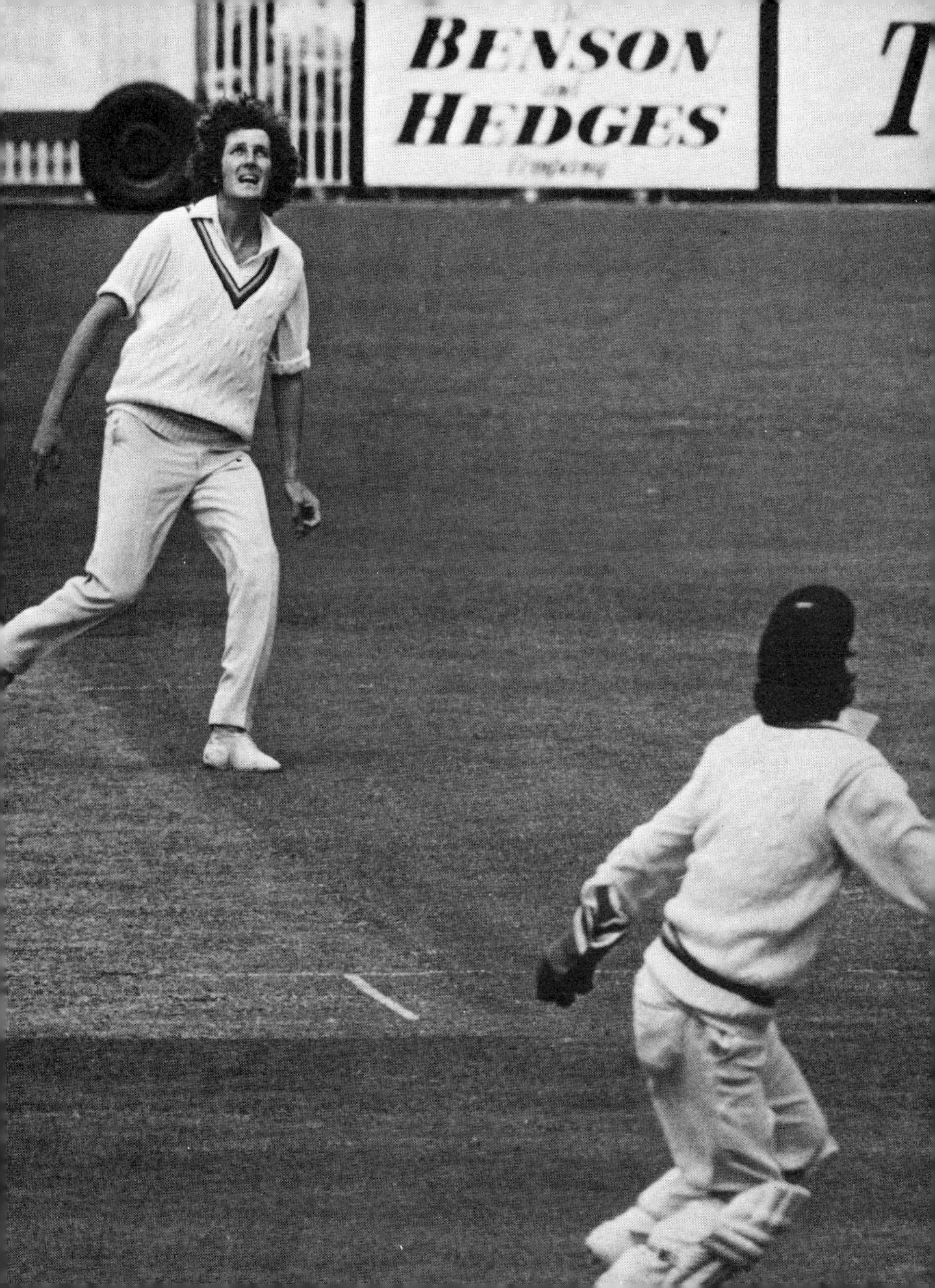
BENSON
HEDGES

cricket *have* helped sharpen up reflexes and speed off the mark.

I'm afraid I'm too critical of my fielders when I'm bowling – when a ball trickles down to third man I'm bellowing: 'Bend your back' when I should be on the way back thinking out the next ball. It's just tenseness on my part in the heat of the moment, but no one should get involved in a slanging match on the field: you need your fielders on your side.

Fielding is one area that's common to all classes of cricket. The club cricketer may have trouble keeping his head still when he's bowling, or he may never master delivering the slower ball, but he should be a good fielder if he's keen on his cricket. Unlike a fast bowler, a good fielder can be manufactured.

Good catching is so vital for the fast bowler. At any level there are hardly any flawless innings. The good batsman normally gives at least a half-chance, and the match often turns on whether the chance is snapped up or not. Look at the great Gary Sobers – you could normally bank on him giving a chance early in his innings, often outside the off stump. If it was dropped, that was normally all you'd get. He never used to give more than one. Look at poor Rick McCosker's dropped catch when Geoff Boycott made his comeback. On the previous tour Rick had taken some blinders close in, but he dropped Boycott off a fairly straightforward chance. If Boycott had gone then, who knows what would have happened to his comeback or England's Ashes prospects?

A fast bowler needs support at the other end. An accurate, nagging bowler like Brian Statham often helped Fred Trueman get wickets because the batsman would have a go at Fred after being frustrated at the other end. That great bowler Derek Underwood helped get me a few wickets because of his remarkable control at the other end. This is where statistics can be very deceiving – I could walk off the field sweating and triumphant, with 5 for 65, while Derek Underwood would plod behind after taking 0 for 50, but his contribution would have been as significant as mine.

A word here on shining the ball to keep the seam clean and dry and one side of the ball shiny so it'll swing. This is where the bowler's team-mates must help. They must lob the ball back into a fielder's hands rather than dropping it short so it bounces and gets scuffed. They must get involved in that ritual of shining the ball religiously. I know it looks a bit too intense sometimes, but a fast bowler needs all the help he can get from the ball as well as his fielders. And when he's finished his bowling stint it's up to him to return the favour and look after the ball for the next bowler. Some players shine the ball better than others. I'm not the greatest at it, while people like David Brown and Steve Perryman at Warwickshire, or Geoff Arnold with Sussex, are very good.

So when you're opening the bowling for your club side or the school first eleven and mid-off keeps dropping the ball when it's thrown back to him, and he continues shelling the ball back to see if you really should take up goal-keeping, give him a rocket. There's no reason why everyone shouldn't look after a new ball, because that helps the fast bowler, which in turn helps the team, which means they get back in the dressing-room quicker . . .

Looking back over the chapters, I find myself thinking: 'Listen to him coming out with all these lectures on discipline. Have you forgotten what an idle devil you were?' No, I certainly haven't, and I assure you I've been guilty of most of the faults in the fast bowling make-up. But I matured in the nick of time, got really stuck into my profession, and now I'm proud to have been England's main strike bowler for so long. But I'm still learning all the time, and there are parts of my game I'm still not happy about and shall keep working at. After all, no one's ever consistently mastered all the arts of fast bowling, and nobody ever will – but it's a lot of fun trying . . .

7 Great Fast Bowlers

The Seventies have been the fast bowlers' decade, and I've been privileged to see all of them in action at close quarters. I'm only glad my Test place hasn't relied on my ability to bat against them, because they're a pretty formidable bunch.

The physical characteristics of my selections have interested me – the four Australians are all magnificently built, with stamina to see them through the most exacting demands of five-day Tests; two of my West Indian choices are comparatively slim; while the English ones are also supple, slight and wiry. Then there's the South African Mike Procter, and I bet nobody's ever kicked sand in his face on the beach . . .

The most fascinating point about my selections is that hardly any of them conform to the classical standards laid down by the coaching manuals. Some have unorthodox deliveries – like Procter – others poor run-ups (Daniel), Andy Roberts has a slightly round-arm action, John Snow isn't completely orthodox at the moment of delivery – but despite these idiosyncrasies, they can bowl fast. Young hopefuls, please note. Don't be coached out of being fast.

I've included my fast bowlers' Test match statistics (up to 1 October 1977), not because I'm a slave to figures but because they say a lot about the striking rate, that vital ratio of wickets to balls delivered. Procter's record in this respect is remarkable – only seven Tests, but they were all against Australia, and if South Africa had stayed in Test cricket, heaven knows what his record would be. Andy Roberts had a faster striking rate when he reached his hundredth Test wicket than any other fast man in history, and only George Lohmann (medium-pace) and Colin Blythe (left-arm spin) had a better record. But the really impressive modern fast men in this respect are Lillee, Thomson and Holding. Only Fred Trueman (49.06), Wes Hall (48.21), and of course Roberts can beat Thommo for the striking rate needed to take 100 Test wickets. Ray Lindwall's figure, for example, is 53.11.

I haven't included maidens in the statistics section because that isn't high on the list of fast bowling priorities. Of course, it's nice to keep a batsman quiet – and in this respect, Old, Snow and Roberts have been very impressive – but our job is to blast men out.

DENNIS LILLEE

Strengths

The greatest fast bowler of my time, he's achieved more movement in the air and off the pitch at high speed than any other quickie since the war. Lillee is proof of the crowd-pulling aura of a fast bowler; he plays to the crowd, they help to lift him, and nobody cares about the slow over-rate when Lillee has the ball. He has a superb high action, with both feet off the ground at that crucial final leap before delivery. This high action means he can bowl a wicked outswinger. A great tactician, his slower ball's a beauty, he can bowl round the wicket, send down surprise fast legbreaks, and off a two-yard run can bowl a very quick bouncer.

Lillee's followthrough is dynamic, he can get really close to the stumps to vary his line of attack and his stamina is tremendous. He made a great recovery from a terrible back injury in 1973 and has bowled for long periods at high speed, for example the Melbourne Centenary Test, where he practically beat England single-handed The fact that he's had to bowl eight-ball overs for nearly a decade in Australia shows how fit he is A great thinker, he paces an over intelligently, interspersing the bouncers with a slower ball, an outswinger, a fast yorker or even just a straight ball.

95

Weaknesses

For a bowler with such high morale, he does seem to get carried away too often. Partly this is due to the Australian crowd goading him, partly due to his own excitable temperament, but there's no doubt he sometimes goes beyond the limit of reasonable aggression. He's a showman, and a great sight when in full flow, but during the Ashes series in Australia in 1974/5 there were times when Lillee went over the top both with the ball and with his tongue – a fascinating contrast to his placid opening partner, Jeff Thomson.

His run-up, though characteristic of his lung-bursting aggression, isn't an ideal one. Of course it suits Lillee, but his flat-footed approach must surely rob him of some of that comfortable litheness that someone like Holding or Thomson enjoys on his run-up.

Test Record

Tests – 32; balls – 8791; runs – 4017; wickets – 171; average – 23.49; striking rate – 51.41.

JEFF THOMSON

Strengths

A great fast bowler with all the right assets – temperament, action, pace, movement and strength – he's proof that unorthodox methods pay off. A magnificent, unique bowling action, with the right arm coming from behind the right knee so that the batsman sees the ball very late. An expert javelin thrower, the enormous propulsion he gets in his delivery comes from his great strength in the trunk and chest. He'll bowl all day without a complaint, he's never had a bad injury from bowling, and his comeback after that terrible shoulder injury in 1976 shows his mental and physical resilience. Many times he must have wondered if he'd ever bowl fast again, but he kept plugging away and came back as fast as ever.

A relaxed, tiptoe approach to the crease, he saves his strength for that gloriously explosive final leap and the ball's delivered from a perfect side-on position. He seems to deliver more unplayable

OPPOSITE *Dennis Lillee*

G

97

balls than other fast bowlers, his fast yorker is frightening, and unlike Lillee he bowls few bouncers. Excellent temperament, enviably philosophical about dropped catches, never gives his captain any trouble.

Weaknesses

Suffers if his rhythm's wrong. In that instant after delivering that ball his eyes often aren't looking straight ahead, they're over in the direction of cover, so that he's not sighting the target properly. His style of just running up and bowling very fast means that if something's missing or his timing's slightly adrift, the margin of error's very small – and the no-balls and wides start coming. When his rhythm's wrong he bowls some spectacular wides, and more than any other great fast bowler Thomson can look ordinary if he's not gelling properly.

Lacks Lillee's guile, but perhaps that'll come with more experience.

Test Record

Tests – 22; balls – 5083; runs – 2607; wickets – 103; average – 25.31; striking rate – 49.35.

GRAHAM McKENZIE

Strengths

McKenzie's last Test match was my first, so I had an early glimpse of a super athlete with a glorious action. His run-up was so relaxed, his movements so graceful, that it often came as a surprise to see the ball rise off the wicket so sharply. The power came from those wide shoulders and that magnificent physique, all from a very short run-up. Modest, quiet and generous, he had the temperament of a Brian Statham. Nothing riled him, the demands of his captain were always met with unselfish good humour, and he'd love to bowl all day.

A great physical fitness man, any fast bowler would do well to

OPPOSITE *Jeff Thomson*

study McKenzie's example of keeping in shape through an arduous decade of fast bowling. His marvellous side-on action meant he could bowl excellent late outswingers, and although he'd be the first to admit his luck in having a first slip like Simpson and a wicketkeeper like Grout in the Australian side for many years, no world-class batsman could feel safe against a bowler who in his prime was a wonderful sight.

Weaknesses

His great strength was his undoing: he was overbowled by too many captains, and the demands of seven-day cricket in England took their toll. His Test match figures don't do him justice, but his decline in his last two series – against South Africa and England – was partly caused by unsympathetic captaincy. Perhaps McKenzie should've complained more often.

He lacked 'devil,' that vital element that makes Lillee so great. Too often he was overgenerous to tail-enders, keeping the ball well up to the bat rather than digging it in short. It wasn't in his nature, but if he'd physically frightened more batsmen his figures would have been even more impressive.

Test Record

Tests – 60; balls – 17,604; Runs – 7328; wickets – 246; average – 29.79; striking rate – 71.56.

ANDY ROBERTS

Strengths

Extremely accurate for a fast bowler, his line is that maddening one for batsman that has him wondering whether to play back or forward, and he'd better make his mind up quickly because the ball's coming through at a hell of a pace. Roberts is a cold-eyed, clinical bowler who hammers away mercilessly at a batsman's weak spot. He never gets over excited if he's hit for several boundar-

OPPOSITE
Graham McKenzie

ies, just keeps bowling, with the highlights a vicious late outswinger and a cleverly disguised slower ball.

Great stamina, and he can bowl two types of bouncer – one the high bouncing type and the other, more dangerous, one that skids through and makes straight for the head.

His remarkable Test striking rate puts him up among the all-time greats, and he can get wickets anywhere – he's bowled superbly in his own country, in England, Australia, and even more impressively considering the slow wickets there, in India and Pakistan.

Weaknesses

Hampshire overbowled him, not surprising really because of his matchwinning qualities, but his arm has got lower in recent seasons. His slightly round-arm action helps his late outswinger but lessens the chance of bowling the one that comes back sharply to middle and leg.

He curtails his followthrough, stopping more abruptly than most fast bowlers. Just imagine how fast he'd be with a really explosive, long followthrough . . .

Test Record

Tests – 25; balls – 6472; runs – 3087; wickets – 122; average – 25.30; striking rate – 53.05.

MICHAEL HOLDING

Strengths

A glorious spectacle in the Thomson/McKenzie mould of fast bowlers. All liquid grace and athleticism, he paces his run-up like the fine 440 runner he is. Very fast through the air because of his high action and powerful impetus from his run-up, he's a godsend to his captain on a lifeless track with no bounce. Holding will clean-bowl Test batsmen on such wickets because of his sheer speed through the air.

For such a young fast bowler, his control is very good, especially

OPPOSITE *Andy Roberts*

his excellent yorker. Very slim for a fast bowler, but his resilience was shown on the tour to England, when he recovered from glandular fever in the early part of the summer to bowl superbly in the last three Tests.

Very penetrative, he managed the rare feat for a quickie of taking fifty Test wickets in a calendar year (1976 – 53 wkts), but even more impressively, the striking rate was an astonishing 46 balls per wicket.

Weaknesses

Although still young and comparatively inexperienced, he's excitable. On his first tour to Australia he refused to bowl once when the umpire turned down one of his appeals, and sat down on the field in tears. Then against the Indians and England he overdid the bouncer, forgetting the maxim that the bouncer's a shock tactic designed to take wickets.

He's had his physical troubles too, a bad shoulder injury twice within eighteen months. Is he durable like Roberts, Thomson and Lillee? Time will tell, but when fully fit, he's a fine sight.

Test Record

Tests – 13; balls – 2909; runs – 1348; wickets – 57; average – 23.64; striking rate – 51.03.

WAYNE DANIEL

Strengths

A massive, frightening sight for a batsman, rather like the West Indian Charlie Griffith a decade earlier, Daniel's the classic example of his country's ability to pluck a really fast bowler out of nowhere. With hardly any experience of first-class cricket under his belt, he learned a lot on the tour to England, smoothed out his run-up, cut down on the no-balls, and terrorized county cricket the following season.

Nobody likes facing Daniel – his huge, brooding presence makes   OPPOSITE *Michael Holding*

you expect high speed, and when the ball arrives you're not disappointed. Bowls a very quick bouncer and a good yorker and is just as dangerous off a short run in the John Player League because of his immense strength and the effort put into his delivery stride.

Weaknesses

A poor, lumbering run-up that only impresses in the last few strides when he's gathering himself for the leap and delivery from a fine side-on position. Almost too muscular, I sometimes wonder how he gets those immense thighs into his flannels – a complete contrast to the graceful Holding.

Still short of experience and cunning, he needs to learn to use the crease, but his dramatic improvement shows he's a quick learner.

Test Record

Tests – 5; balls – 788; runs – 381; wickets – 15; average – 25.40; striking rate – 52.53.

JOHN SNOW

Strengths

When he felt like it, a top-class performer. A fine controlled run-up which led to a whippy delivery, (it often reminded me of the act of pulling back and firing an arrow). Everything was done smoothly, at a deceptively fast pace. His followthrough was first-class, with his right arm almost touching the ground.

On my first tour to Australia, Snow was the best bowler in the world. He was the strike force, with the accuracy to be a stock bowler as well if Ray Illingworth wanted the game kept tight. Many thought he should have gone to Australia again four years later with Mike Denness, and remembering how he bowled against the Aussies when recalled a year later by Tony Greig, who could argue?

His control was superb – if necessary he could deliver the same

OPPOSITE *Wayne Daniel*

type of ball over after over, hammering away just short of driveable length and not short enough for the hook or the cut – every delivery at speed. I remember him bowling like that against the great Barry Richards on a perfect wicket in South Africa. For six overs, Richards had to play the same shot to every ball – he couldn't get him off the square – and at lunch Richards showed me his right hand, which had been badly jarred by Snow's constant attack. It was a great piece of defensive batting by a master batsman, but a marvellous display of controlled hostility by Snow.

Snow's Test record is impressive. Essentially a big-occasion player, he took wickets all over the world and was a real handful on the fast, bouncy tracks in West Indies and Australia.

Snow's lethargic manner's fooled many a good batsman. His breakback from the off could be sharp and devastatingly late, and he specialized in the low, skidding bouncers perfected by bowlers like Roberts and Statham.

A naturally fit, slim man, he was never seriously troubled by injuries.

Weaknesses

Temperament. If he couldn't be bothered, it needed a skilful, strong captain to make him snap out of it. Although a conscientious hard worker in the nets when developing his craft, he later relied more on natural ability than hard work. Once his dander was up, Snow was magnificently hostile, but he didn't have the Fred Trueman philosophy of expecting a wicket every delivery, and many times Snow would rather mope on the boundary edge than run up and bowl. If he'd possessed the high optimistic morale of say, Dennis Lillee, what a bowler he'd have been!

Ray Illingworth got more our of Snow than any other skipper. Early in that successful tour of Australia, Ray made it clear that if Snow didn't toe the line he'd be on the next plane back. As a result, Snow never bowled better in a series.

Technically, Snow veered away too much at the moment of delivery and his feet weren't in the correct position at that instant, but he developed a good, high whippy action to counteract that.

OPPOSITE *John Snow*

Tests – 49; balls – 12,027; runs – 5387; wickets – 202; average – 26.67; striking rate – 59.94.

CHRIS OLD

Strengths

Excellent, textbook technique. Chris looks over the left shoulder to get a sighting when about to deliver the ball, he keeps his head still in his approach and delivery, he gets side-on, bowls a splendid outswinger and uses the crease well. With more experience he's corrected slight technical errors – he used to splay his left foot towards second slip rather than fine leg just before delivery – but that's been ironed out and he's now the ideal model for an ambitious fast bowler at school or club level.

Quicker than he looks, his whippy action catches the batsman by surprise. He thinks about his game, has a good tactical memory and can vary his line of attack against a class batsman and a tail-ender effortlessly in one over. Like most Yorkshiremen, he's very accurate and hates giving runs away. Because of his fine action, he's still pacy off his shortened run in limited-over matches.

An unlucky bowler, he's often helped me take wickets because his tight control has made the batsman rashly look for runs at my end.

Weaknesses

Lacks confidence for such a talented all-round cricketer. Gets very nervous before a Test, often for reasons he just can't put his finger on. With his slight physique, he's had his injury problems, gets depressed and has to be persuaded he's fitter than he thinks. Tony Greig had to bully him to keep going in the Melbourne Centenary Test, and he needs sympathetic yet firm handling.

Test Record

OPPOSITE *Chris Old*

Tests – 33; balls – 6024; runs – 3032; wickets – 102; average – 29.72; striking rate – 59.06.

MIKE PROCTER

Strengths

Like myself, his very unorthodoxy is a great asset. Batsmen never know what's coming to them as he whirls in off that long run and bowls off the wrong foot.

His stock delivery is a huge inswinger – his speed doesn't leave time for the ball to do anything else – yet the skilful way he bowls round the wicket helps to vary his line of attack. His speed comes from his immensely strong chest and shoulders and terrific arm pace generated from a magnificently hostile run. He really sprints in, and I can tell you it's a disconcerting sight if you're at the far end with just a lump of wood in your hand to defend yourself.

He's not a tall man, but that final leap just before delivery gets him bounce. An inspirational bowler, on his day he's everything that a fast bowler should be – dynamic, penetrative, with that priceless asset of stamina, all the more admirable considering the bad knee injuries he's suffered in the past.

Procter's great morale means that he never knows when he's licked. Captaincy seems to have improved his bowling and he has the intelligence not to overbowl himself. A naturally talented cricketer, the fact that he's also a fine batsman helps his bowling because he understands the mental pressures a batsman goes through at certain stages in an innings, and Procter the bowler can spot important things.

Weaknesses

The strain on his admittedly magnificent physique must be immense, especially in a crowded English season with all the demands placed on his batting, captaincy and strike bowling ability. The strain comes not only in that unorthodox delivery but in his approach to the wicket. He's a *sprinting* fast bowler, a rare breed, and I just hope he can keep it up for a few more years. Perhaps he'll then take up offbreaks full-time, and judging by the wickets he's already taken with that style, he'll carve himself out a new career when he's about thirty-five. Lucky man, talented man . . .

OPPOSITE *Mike Pocter*

112

Tests – 7; balls – 1514; runs – 616; wickets – 41; average – 15.02; striking rate – 36.93.

LEN PASCOE

Strengths

A very impressive replacemnt for Lillee on the 1977 tour to England, he was distinctly sharp off a short run-up. He bustles in, building up momentum, and lets the ball go at just the right time, saving the real energy for the final explosion. His strong physique helps him turn his trunk from the sideways position to face the batsman at the moment of delivery in the shortest possible time.

A willing worker, he bowled a lot of overs in his first Test series and looked a real prospect, despite a niggling hamstring injury that he shrugged offf.

Weaknesses

The obvious ones in a young, strong quickie; he concentrates on just running up and letting the ball go at speed, on all-out attack. With more experience he'll learn variety and stop getting rattled and resorting to the bouncer when all else fails. But with that fine, compact action, he's definitely one to watch . . .

Test Record

Tests – 3; balls – 825; runs – 363; wickets – 13; average – 27.92; striking rate – 63.54.

BOB WILLIS

And for all you readers wondering when I'm going to cast aside my pretence at modesty, here are my vital statistics.

Test Record

Tests – 29; balls – 5457; runs – 2746; wickets – 105; average – 26.15; striking rate – 51.97.

Bob Willis